CITIES OF THE
WORLD

VANCOUVER

BY BARBARA RADCLIFFE ROGERS AND
STILLMAN D. ROGERS

CHILDREN'S PRESS®
A Division of Scholastic Inc.
New York Toronto London Auckland Sydney
Mexico City New Delhi Hong Kong
Danbury, Connecticut

CONSULTANTS

Laura Serena
Manager, Travel Media Relations
Tourism Vancouver

Linda Cornwell
Coordinator of School Quality and Professional Improvement
Indiana State Teachers Association

Project Editor: Downing Publishing Services
Design Director: Karen Kohn & Associates, J. Breslin
Photo Researcher: Jan Izzo

Library of Congress Cataloging-in-Publication Data
Rogers, Barbara Radcliffe
    Vancouver / by Barbara Radcliffe Rogers and Stillman D. Rogers.
      p. cm. — (Cities of the world)
Includes bibliographical references and index.
Summary: Describes the history, culture, daily life, food, people, sports,
and points of interest in the largest city in British Columbia, Canada.
    ISBN 0-516-22186-8 (lib. bdg.)   0-516-25961-X (pbk.)
    1. Vancouver (B.C.)—Juvenile literature. [1. Vancouver (B.C.) 2. Canada] I.Rogers,
Stillman, 1939- II. Title. III. Cities of the world (New York, N.Y.)
    F1089.5.V22 R56 2001
    971.1'2—dc21

                            00-060122

TABLE OF CONTENTS

GATEWAY TO THE

Vancouver is Canada's gateway to the Pacific Ocean. A transportation center since its earliest days, the city's first growth spurt began when it became the terminus for Canada's transcontinental railway. Today, as gateway to the world's fastest-growing trade markets around the Pacific Rim, Vancouver is the largest port on the entire west coast of North America.

Vancouver's Pacific gate swings in two directions. While goods from Canada head to Pacific markets, people and products from Asia have arrived through the same port. Many of them go no farther. They are attracted by Vancouver's gentle climate, economic opportunities, and beautiful setting.

Below: A woman sitting on a bench in a Vancouver park next to a statue of a sitting woman

It would be a mistake, however, to think that all of Vancouver's new arrivals have come from Asia. The city's mild climate and beautiful position between the mountains and sea attract Canadians from all corners of the country, especially from the cold northern provinces and territories. Compared with their bitter winters of ice and snow, Vancouver seems almost like the tropics!

Above: The seawall and Lions Gate Bridge in Stanley Park
Right: A young boy playing in the leaves in a Vancouver park

Vancouver's people are not the only diverse thing about the city. Its natural setting also makes it unusual. Snow-capped mountains are so close to the sea that people can ski in the morning and sail in the afternoon without ever leaving the city. Man-made and natural wonders are almost side by side in Vancouver. Streets of lovely old homes have modern sparkling towers of glass and steel as their neighbors. Old and new blend in an exciting and ever-changing swirl.

THE MANY FACES OF VANCOUVER

For its entire history, immigrants have helped shape the city and colored Vancouver life with their varied cultures and traditions. In its earliest years, the land was shared by First Nations Peoples (as Canadians call their Native Americans) and settlers from the British Isles. The British settlers set the customs and traditions that would predominate, even after many other cultures joined them there.

In the 1850s, the first Chinese arrived from the gold fields of California, drawn by the lure of gold discovered on the Fraser River. A second wave arrived in the 1880s to lay tracks for the Canadian Pacific Railway. A third group came after Hong Kong was turned over to China in 1997. Many of Hong Kong's wealthiest merchants and bankers relocated in Vancouver.

In the late 1800s, Japanese fishermen settled along the rich fishing grounds of the Fraser River Delta. A large community of Sikhs from India also emigrated to Vancouver. Jews fleeing oppression in Eastern Europe soon joined them.

Like the Chinese, each of these groups gathered into its own few blocks, creating a series of ethnic neighborhoods where people who shared a common language, religion, and culture could support one another—often in the face of poverty and poor treatment. Living conditions were crowded and city government often ignored the health and safety of the newcomers who crowded into inadequate housing.

A young child in Vancouver's Chinatown

Each of these groups has taken its hard-won place in modern Vancouver. Today, Chinatown is a colorful, cosmopolitan, downtown neighborhood where tourists and Vancouverites mingle in restaurants, bakeries, markets, and shops. Japantown centers around its big food market. Little India's Main Street is lined with shops selling jewelry and bright

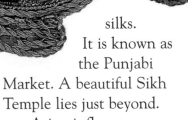

silks. It is known as the Punjabi Market. A beautiful Sikh Temple lies just beyond.

Asian influences continue to grow, as people whose ancestors were born in Vietnam, Cambodia, Thailand, and elsewhere arrive. Not all Asians are immigrants. More than half the foreign visitors who come to Vancouver each year are Asian, and it is not unusual to see signs in shop windows welcoming them in their own languages. Some of the major hotels are owned by Japanese companies. So many Asian students have attended the city's schools and colleges that more than 20,000 of their graduates live in Hong Kong alone.

While Asians have the most visible of Vancouver's ethnic communities, Greeks, Italians, and others have neighborhoods where churches, shops, and restaurants reflect their own cultural roots.

This customer at the Punjabi Market can choose from items such as the ornament shown above or the silk sari bag shown at right.

A CITY ON THE WATER

To understand Vancouver, we must picture its setting. It is at the edge of Canada's most mountainous region, the great range known as the Western Cordillera. Not far from the city, mountains rise 7,000 to 13,000 feet (2,134 to 3,962 meters), protecting Vancouver from icy north winds and giving it a wet, gentle climate.

On the western side of Vancouver, across the Strait of Georgia, is Vancouver Island, the largest of the hundreds of islands strewn along the Pacific shore of British Columbia. Vancouver Island and the Queen Charlotte Islands farther north, along with many smaller islands, create a barrier between the mainland coast and the Pacific Ocean. The sheltered water that stretches from Alaska all the way south to the U.S.

A view of the mountains from Howe Sound

A carving of a killer whale at the Cowichan Native Heritage Centre in Duncan, near Victoria

state of Washington is called the Inside Passage. These protected waters have provided a safe route for boats and ships since the native peoples first fished there.

The Fraser River, 850 miles (1,368 kilometers) long, flows westward from the Rocky Mountains, meeting the sea in a broad delta at Vancouver. More than 1.9 million people live in this valley and delta. Most of them live in Vancouver, which is the most important commercial and cultural center in the province of British Columbia. The sea, the mountains, and the river affect Vancouver's weather, its economy, and even the way people there spend their leisure time.

A sailboat in the Strait of Georgia

VANCOUVER, NATURALLY

Although Vancouver is filled with bright new modern buildings, its tall skyline is dwarfed by the mountains that rise from the shore to its north. Water nearly surrounds the downtown area. This combination of mountains and sea is beautiful— Vancouver is often compared to Rio de Janeiro and Hong Kong as one of the world's most spectacular cities. Nature's wonders are very close to the city.

Hundreds of sea lions from as far away as Alaska and Baja California (in Mexico) gather each spring at the mouth of the Fraser River to feast on salmon. The nearby Reifel Bird Sanctuary, also on the Fraser Delta, attracts huge flocks of migrating birds each spring and fall. As many as 350 kinds of birds have been seen. Flocks of as many as 10,000 beautiful white snow geese stop there.

In Brackendale, north of the city, thousands of bald eagles can be seen in the winter, the most ever counted at one place in North America. Like the sea lions, the eagles feast on the salmon that have returned to spawn in the river.

At Lighthouse Park, trails lead through a northern rain forest, where giant Douglas fir trees grow. In Stanley Park stands a red cedar tree that the National Geographic Society has identified as the largest in the world. It is more than 90 feet (30 m) around.

Two deep gorges cut by rushing rivers in North Vancouver are crossed by swinging suspension footbridges.

Bald eagles like this one come to Brackendale to feast on salmon in the Fraser River.

"I survived"
the Capilano Bridge

The Capilano Suspension Bridge is the longest and highest bridge of its kind in the world. It gives new meaning to the words "suspension" and "suspense" as it swings over the rushing waters of the 230-foot- (70-m-) deep Capilano Canyon in North Vancouver.

PLANES, TRAINS, AND BOATS

Ever since its early days as the western terminus for the Canadian Pacific Railway, Vancouver has been a "train" city. In addition to the transcontinental trains, visitors to Vancouver have their choice of several scenic train rides.

BC Rail travels through the ranch country and E&N Rail is one of the most scenic rides in the West, as it goes along the shores of Vancouver Island. The Rocky Mountaineer travels from Vancouver to the Rocky Mountains on a two-day scenic ride. The train travels only by day, and passengers can see the mountains from glass-enclosed sky-dome cars.

The Royal Hudson steam train travels to Squamish, combining the ride with a return trip by boat. The Pacific Starlight Dinner Train runs each evening along the shore of Howe Sound. Its passengers eat dinner on board as the beautiful coastal and mountain scenery moves past their windows.

*A Pacific Star-
light Dinner Train
souvenir*

*A Royal Hudson steam
train engineer cap*

In the city itself, people commute to work on the SkyTrain, a completely automated commuter rail system that runs 18 miles (29 km) on a scenic high track. The SeaBus, the only water bus system of its kind in the world, takes commuters across the busy Burrard Inlet to North Vancouver. A century ago, the Burrard Inlet was so quiet that anyone summoning the ferry (a rowboat then), could just yell across the water.

A fleet of tiny ferries shuttles around the shores of False Creek, on the south side of Vancouver. It stops at Yaletown, Granville Island, and Science World. Large car ferries also go to Victoria, but the fastest way is by a small floatplane. These airplanes, which take off and land right on the water, have their "airport" at a dock right beside Vancouver's downtown cruise port.

Left: The Royal Hudson steam train traveling through North Vancouver
Below: The BC ferry terminal on Horseshoe Bay

It's hard to believe that the large city whose high-rise buildings stand above the Strait of Georgia is scarcely 125 years old. It is one of the world's youngest important cities. But long before there was a city there, First Nations Peoples fished in the rich waters of the Fraser River, and built small villages on its shore.

British navigator and explorer George Vancouver discovered Burrrard Inlet in 1792 and claimed the area for Britain.

ROOM FOR EVERYONE

For more than 5,000 years, First Nations Peoples lived in these small settlements on the banks of the Fraser River. These Coast Salish peoples included many small tribes who shared similar languages and customs. A highly developed people, they built wooden houses, made beautiful wood carvings, and wove baskets from the bark of red cedar trees.

The Salish followed the fish and game as seasons changed. They hollowed out red cedar logs to make canoes for fishing and trading. They traded shells, slaves, ivory, hides, and baskets with other tribes. The Europeans who came to trade did not make war on the First Nations Peoples, but European diseases killed whole villages of them.

In 1792, Captain George Vancouver found and charted the large harbor called Burrard Inlet and claimed the area for Britain. Sixteen years later, Simon Fraser followed a river he thought was the Columbia River and came to the Strait of Georgia. The river he followed was later named the Fraser River, in his honor. Neither of these first European encounters with the area led to settlement.

The Fraser River was named for Simon Fraser (above), who followed the river sixteen years after George Vancouver discovered Burrard Inlet.

Traffic on Vancouver's Fraser River

HERE TO STAY

It wasn't until 1827 that the Hudson's Bay Company built a fur-trading post and fort at Fort Langley. Although it was the first settlement in the area, it was only for trade with the First Nations Peoples. Settlers were discouraged. But there was no stopping the flood of 30,000 prospectors who rushed to the region when gold was discovered in the sands of the Fraser River in 1858. Britain was fearful that with so many people pouring in from California and other states, the United States might claim the area. So Britain created the Crown Colony of British Columbia in 1858. A site on the Fraser River was chosen as a capital and named New Westminster.

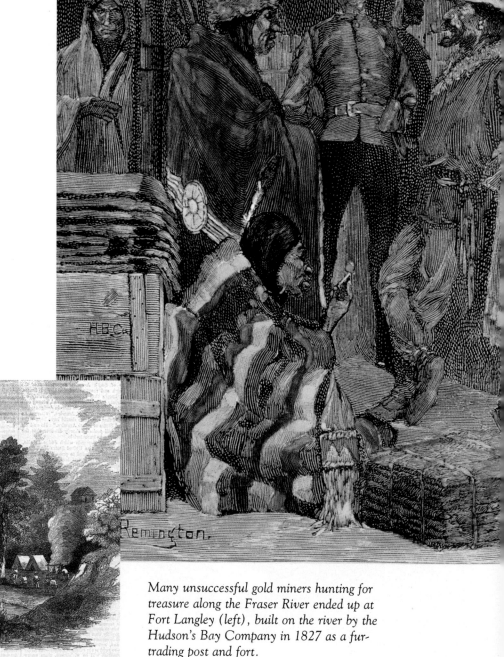

FORT LANGLEY, FRAZER'S RIVER.

Many unsuccessful gold miners hunting for treasure along the Fraser River ended up at Fort Langley (left), built on the river by the Hudson's Bay Company in 1827 as a fur-trading post and fort.

This colored woodcut of a Frederic Remington illustration depicts a Hudson's Bay Company trading store.

The announcement in 1884 that the Canadian Pacific Railway had decided to have its West Coast terminus at the end of the Burrard Inlet brought a sudden burst of growth. Other small villages had grown up on the coast, and one of them, Granville, incorporated itself as the City of Vancouver in 1886. In spite of a fire that destroyed all but six buildings, the city prospered. City Hall was set up in a tent and the enthusiastic city council rebuilt the city and even created its first park, Stanley Park.

A totem pole in Stanley Park

THE NEW CITY GROWS

The first Europeans had come to the shores of the Burrard Inlet as fur trappers and traders, doing business through the Hudson's Bay Company. The abundant salmon that had fed the First Nations Peoples attracted the next wave of settlers. They set up fisheries along the shores, at first drying and salting the fish. By the 1870s, canneries were packing and processing the fish for shipment.

The vast untouched forests of huge trees brought settlers who saw the trees as a way to wealth. Thousands of acres of trees were sold to timbermen to be cut down and shipped away.

All this new industry meant that even more people were needed to work in the factories and wood-

This 1880s picture of a wharf along the North Pacific Coast was one of many from which thousands of acres of trees were shipped as timber from the Pacific Northwest.

Between 1866 and 1873, whalers like this one killed 81 giant humpback whales in the Strait of Georgia. By 1906, every last humpback whale had been killed.

lands. First Nations Peoples, whose whole way of life had been taken away by the new settlers, became the first workers. Chinese workers, brought from China to build the railroad, were hired at low wages to fill more of these new jobs. Many other people came from Europe and from other parts of Canada. They established farms to provide the growing population with food.

The population grew steadily, from about 1,000 in 1886 to 27,000 only fifteen years later. In the next ten years, the population increased to nearly five times that many. The great forests that George Vancouver and Simon Fraser saw had been cut down to make way for a new city.

The forests were not the only casualty as the city began to rise. The Strait of Georgia once teemed with sea life, including as many as 500 humpback whales. These huge creatures returned each year to one of the world's richest and most productive coastal ecosystems. Between 1866 and 1873, 81 of these giants were killed by whalers and turned into whale oil. By 1906, every last whale had been killed. Meanwhile, commercial fisheries were quickly catching all the halibut, salmon, sturgeon, and other desirable fish, until almost none remained. One by one, lesser sea life was targeted and removed, until the once-fine marine ecosystem was ruined forever.

A MARKET FOR THE WORLD

The opening of the Panama Canal in 1914 increased the demand for western Canadian lumber. The logging industry boomed. As Canada's western prairies were opened to agriculture, Vancouver became an important port for shipping and exporting grain—especially wheat—to the United States, Europe, and Asia. Vancouver's huge natural harbor in the Burrard Inlet was becoming the busiest port in Canada.

This photo of downtown Vancouver was taken in 1939.

A 1940 picture of Granville Street, Vancouver's principal shopping area at the time

These exports continued to grow during and after World War I, until 25 percent of all Canadian wheat exports were passing through the port. The port and the city around it grew until the Great Depression of the 1930s slowed the growth of the city as the demand for exports shrank and jobs became scarce. Until the 1950s, times were hard.

The city of the 1940s and 1950s was still small, with no high-rise buildings, but that was about to change. From 1945 to the early 1990s, the population nearly tripled, and the city shot upward to make room for all the people.

In the 1940s and 1950s, Vancouver began to build high-rise buildings to accommodate its growing population.

Friends having fun at Expo 86

BALANCING ON THE RIM

From an economy based on the sale and processing of fish, lumber, and other raw materials, Vancouver expanded to other businesses, which grew and prospered quickly. Its position as a major Pacific Coast port led Vancouver to do more and more business with the Pacific Rim countries. When Expo 86 was held in Vancouver to promote the city and the area, more than twice as many people attended as were expected. This exposition helped turn the city into a major international trade, banking, and business center.

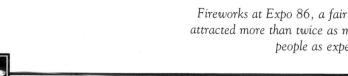

Fireworks at Expo 86, a fair that attracted more than twice as many people as expected

Vancouver's many high-rise office buildings attest to the city's position as a banking and finance center for the entire Pacific Rim.

Trade with Japan, China, and other Asian countries has continued to expand. The city has become a center of banking and finance for the entire Pacific Rim. The central part of the city, on the west end of the Burrard Peninsula, has blossomed with many high-rise office buildings. The city's continuing role as a major international center for banking and trade seems certain.

LAND

Some people of Asian ancestry who live in Vancouver call their city Lotus Land for its love of good living, especially fine food. Vancouver has become a center for culinary arts, influenced by its many immigrant populations. It is also a center for the performing and fine arts, with dozens of theaters, museums, and galleries.

FOODS AND FESTIVALS

Vancouverites think their city has the perfect combination: chefs from every cuisine in the world and all the fresh ingredients they could possibly need. They are right. The sea, the rich farmlands of the Okanagan Valley, and the city's position as a shipping center combine to give chefs an endless supply of foods to work with.

Like the city itself, Vancouver's menus include and blend traditions from all over the world, creating a unique Western Canadian style of its own. Nearly every cuisine imaginable is represented in Vancouver restaurants. Diners can even get a typical dinner of smoked salmon prepared by First Nations Peoples and served in a cedar longhouse.

One of the best ways to sample the foods of all Vancouver's different peoples is at the many ethnic and neighborhood festivals that take place throughout the year.

Participants in the Kits Day Parade, held in June

Left: A woman in traditional costume taking part in a Chinese New Year parade in Vancouver

Below: A First Nations Peoples powwow

A Calendar of Vancouver's Ethnic Festivals

January (or early February): Chinese New Year,
with a parade
April: Basakhi Day, the Indian New Year
May: Sikh Sports Festival
June: Canadian International
Dragon Boat Festival
July: Caribbean Days Festival
July: Greek Days
July: Italian Days
August: Squamish Band (First Nations Peoples) Powwow
August: Powell Street Festival (Japanese)
November: Festival of Lights in Little India

A lion in the
Chinese New
Year parade

DOWNTOWN VANCOUVER

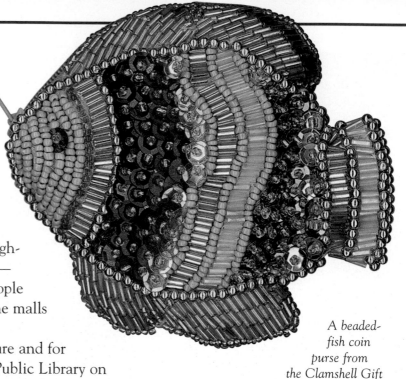

Unlike many cities, where people who work in the downtown offices go home to shop and play in the suburbs at night, Vancouver's downtown stays active and lively until late every evening. People live in the heart of the city and visit the cafés, parks, restaurants, and shops that make the business area a neighborhood of its own. Shopping in downtown Vancouver—especially along Robson Street—is so enjoyable that people come in from the suburbs to shop, instead of going to the malls outside of town.

Vancouver is known for its cutting-edge architecture and for buildings with interesting shapes. The new Vancouver Public Library on Library Square, for example, is partly surrounded by a narrow building that reminds everyone of Rome's Colosseum. Other striking modern buildings that help make Vancouver a beautiful city are the Ford Centre for the Performing Arts and the Vancouver Art Gallery.

A beaded-fish coin purse from the Clamshell Gift Shop in Vancouver

The Vancouver Trade and Convention Centre has five distinctive towers that were designed to look like sails.

The Vancouver Public Library at Library Square is partly surrounded by a narrow, round building that reminds people of Rome's Colosseum.

Visitors arriving on one of the many cruise boats that use Vancouver as a port of call have an unforgettable first view of the harbor as they approach the Vancouver Trade and Convention Centre. Originally built as the Canadian Pavilion for Expo 86, the white building is topped by five white towers, designed to look like the billowing sails of a ship.

VANCOUVER'S NEIGHBORHOODS

Like most large cities, Vancouver is divided into neighborhoods. City planners count 22 of these urban communities within the city. Some are small residential areas, but others have such distinct characteristics that they seem like separate towns within the city.

The West End is Canada's most densely populated area. It is second only to Manhattan (in New York City) in all of North America for the number of people per square mile. At the beginning of the twentieth century, it was home to Vancouver's wealthiest families. A few of their grand old mansions remain among the apartment buildings, shops, and eating places. More than 50 restaurants line one seven-block stretch of Denman Street.

Neon street signs blink in two languages in Chinatown, which has spilled over into neighboring Strathcona, the city's oldest residential section. Vancouver's Chinatown ranks with those in New York, San Francisco, and Toronto as one of the continent's largest Chinese neighborhoods. It is filled with lively food markets, restaurants, noodle shops, and pharmacies selling Chinese medicinal herbs. Chinatown centers around Pender and Keefer Streets.

Yaletown was once a district of warehouses and rowdy bars but has now been "gentrified" into an arts community, with theaters, art galleries, and loft apartments filling the old buildings. The 204-acre (83-hectare) fairground of Expo 86 is now one of North America's largest apartment complexes.

Cups like this one can be found in the shops of Vancouver's Chinatown.

False Creek splits Yaletown from the fast-growing, hip Granville Island. On weekends, Vancouver residents cross False Creek on little ferries to shop at Granville Island Market and in the boutiques and galleries nearby. Modern condos and townhouses reach up the side of Mount Pleasant, which rises behind it.

Japantown, also called "Little Tokyo," lies along Powell Street. It includes blocks of shops and the Sunrise Market, where Japanese vegetables and other foods are sold. This neighborhood was larger before World War II, when the Canadian government moved most of its residents to internment camps and took away their property.

Shaughnessy is actually three neighborhoods, all built in the early 1900s by the Canadian Pacific Railway for the city's wealthiest social elite. Its well-kept homes are still surrounded by gardens, and still home to the wealthy

A traditional gate marks the entrance to Vancouver's Chinatown.

Vancouverites and tourists shopping and dining at the Granville Island Market

residents of the city. Its shops reflect the pocketbooks and tastes of the people who live there.

Little Italy, in East Vancouver, now includes many other ethnic communities. It is an area where new immigrants and students can afford to live. In its relaxed streets are many cafés and places to buy Italian ice cream, along with a lively center for the performing arts.

THE ARTS

Few cities have a busier calendar of theater, music, art, and entertainment events than Vancouver. It would be impossible to see or take part in everything offered during Vancouver's "Entertainment Season," which runs from October through April. Vancouver and Montreal share the position of Canada's dance capital. Vancouver has eighteen professional dance companies whose performances range from traditional Japanese styles to Russian ballet.

Bramwell Tovey conducted the Vancouver Symphony Orchestra along with more than 6,000 student musicians in May 2000.

Vancouver has its own Symphony Orchestra, as well as the only remaining city radio orchestra in North America, the Vancouver CBC Radio Orchestra. Each year, the city hosts the outstanding Du Maurier International Jazz Festival, as well as festivals of folk music and chamber music. Vancouver is a major center for Taiko drumming. It combines Japanese traditions with African and Latin American sounds, creating a musical style that seems to represent the city's own lively artistic mix.

More than thirty-two professional theater groups keep Vancouver's stages busy, even though the city has more than twenty places for them to perform. The Fringe Festival and the New Play Festival are both major annual events. The city operates three major theaters that host concerts and shows, including many touring Broadway shows.

The Arts Club began in 1964 and now has two theaters. Many well-known performers, including Michael J. Fox, got their start at the Arts Club Theatre.

One theater, the Firehall Arts Centre, was founded with the single purpose of presenting theater that represents Canada's cultural diversity.

Vancouver is an appropriate place for it to be.

The annual Vancouver International Film Festival, held each fall, presents more than 300 films from at least 50 countries and is attended by more than 100,000 movie fans. Vancouver is also an important film and television production center, ranking third to New York and Los Angeles. The city has been seen in movies and television shows, where it has been used to represent such varied settings as Africa, China, Vietnam, and even French vineyards! The popular television series, *The X Files*, was shot in Vancouver. Visitors look for the big white production trailers parked on the city's streets.

They can even call a special hot line to watch movie stars in action.

Although Vancouver is famous for its performing arts, few people realize that it is also a major literary center. More than 250 titles are published there each year. It is the cultural center for the more than 1,500 authors who live in the province of British Columbia. It is home to W. P. Kinsella, whose book *Shoeless Joe* was made into the movie *Field of Dreams*. With all these writers, it is not surprising that Vancouver has more book readers than any other place in Canada. Each year, the city hosts the Vancouver International Writers and Readers Festival, which draws 12,000 people.

This group of junior-high-school students represents Vancouver's cultural diversity.

VANCOUVER AT PLAY

Canada's Mike Weir lining up his ball during the Greater Vancouver Open

People in Vancouver spend more money on sports equipment, such as running shoes and boats, than people in any other Canadian city. On weekends, holidays, evenings, and even during their lunch hours, Vancouver's residents like to be active. They walk, run, and bicycle along city streets and around beautiful Stanley Park. A flat 5.6-mile (9-km) paved path borders the water along the seawall that surrounds the park. Vancouver's mild climate makes it a good year-round place for walkers and cyclists.

More than 180 free public tennis courts in the city are used year-round, and more than a dozen golf courses are in the city or close by. Since 1996, Vancouver has hosted the PGA tour at the Greater Vancouver Open, played in August. It is held at the Northview Golf & Country Club course, designed by Arnold Palmer. Some of golf's greatest stars compete in this event.

Within less than 30 minutes of the city, skiers have their choice of three mountains, each of which is lighted for night skiing. One of these, Grouse Mountain, is also a

Golf tees

A skier on Whistler Mountain

favorite of climbers, who try to beat the latest time record up the steep 45-degree "Grouse Grind."

Of course, water sports are literally all around the city. Sailboats glide across the water and bright kayaks explore the shores. Kayaks, which can be rented on Granville Island and English Bay, are based on the design of *baidarkas*, used by the First Nations Peoples of coastal Alaska. Close to town, kayakers can paddle along Indian Arm, a fjord that stretches into the heart of the Coastal Range mountains.

Underwater, SCUBA divers can see wolf eels, octopus, and bright red coral. Nearby shipwrecks still turn up occasional bits of sunken treasure. Of course, fishing is a popular sport with Vancouverites, who fish for salmon in the rivers and for saltwater fish from any of the many boats that leave Granville Island and other places along the shore.

Stanley Park is a favorite place for Vancouverites to walk, run, and bicycle. Along the way, they also enjoy the beauty of the Rose Garden.

SPECTATOR SPORTS

For such a young city, Vancouver has a long tradition of local team sports, and people there support their teams with enthusiasm. The Vancouver Canucks, members of the National Hockey League, are the city's pride. In 1995, the Canucks came within a single goal of winning the Stanley Cup, which would have been especially fitting, since the coveted prize was established by a Vancouverite, the same person who founded Stanley Park.

Peter Schaefer (number 72) of the Vancouver Canucks has just scored a goal against Anaheim Mighty Ducks goalie Guy Hebert in this March 2000 hockey game.

Two Long Legacies

Vancouver's Stanley Park is named for Governor General Frederick Arthur, Lord Stanley of Preston. He was an avid fan of ice hockey and in 1893–1894 he donated the Stanley Cup (left). It is the oldest trophy awarded to professional athletes in North America. The trophy originally went to the winner of a play-off between Canadian teams. In 1926, it was taken over by the National Hockey League.

The year before, in 1994, the BC Lions had become Canadian Football League champions. Their home stadium is at the 60,000-seat domed BC Place. People from the United States who come up from Seattle and elsewhere to see their games notice several differences between U.S. and Canadian football. In Canada, play is limited to three downs, instead of four, and the field is longer and wider. This means that football games have more passing and faster play than their counterparts south of the border.

Across the street from BC Place, at the new GM Place, the Vancouver Grizzlies played their first game in 1996. They are a National Basketball Association franchise. It did not take long for people in Vancouver to become fanatical fans of their new team.

In contrast to these state-of-the-art modern stadiums, the 6,500-seat Nat Bailey Stadium seems old fashioned and quaint, with real grass and a manually operated scoreboard. Vancouver baseball fans love its traditional charm—

and the local team that plays there. The AAA team, called the Vancouver Canadians, are members of the Pacific Coast League and have been playing at Nat Bailey since 1978. To make their team even more accessible to fans, the stadium has a policy of free admission to the last two innings of play in every game.

The Vancouver Whitecaps represent their city in soccer, and are

members of the American Professional Soccer League.

Canada's largest spectator sport event, the Molson Indy, is run each September on the streets around the end of False Creek, near Science World. More than 160,000 people line the streets for three days to watch these high-performance racing cars.

Rookie driver Juan Montoya of Colombia speeds through the rain at the Molson Indy in 1999.

No city loves visitors more than Vancouver. The city makes it very easy for people to get around, with buses, trains, and boats that are fun to ride. The SkyTrain brings people from the railway station to downtown, running part of the way on tracks elevated above street level. Passengers have a beautiful view of the city. Vancouver is especially welcoming to people with limited mobility and has been called the "most accessible city in the world" by a newsletter for disabled people. Public transportation is equipped for wheelchairs, and more than 14,000 wheelchair ramps make sidewalks accessible all over the city.

A BUSY WATERFRONT

Many boats use Vancouver's busy harbor. More than thirty large transport ships come and go each day, in addition to giant white cruise ships. Colorful little sailboats, fishing boats, and cruisers are owned by local families. Passengers enjoy the scenic ferry ride to North Vancouver across the Burrard Inlet. Watching boats on the waterfront is one of the locals' favorite pastimes.

Many visitors get their first view of Vancouver from the sea. They arrive at the sparkling new cruise ship terminal, located at the Vancouver Trade and Convention Centre, which was the Canadian Pavilion for Expo 86. Others like to begin with a bird's-eye view of the city from the top of another modern building, the Harbour Centre. A glass elevator whisks passengers more than 500 feet (152 m) into the air to the big saucer-shaped observation platform called The Lookout! Along with a 360-degree view over the city, the water, and the mountains, the center has a multi-image show on Vancouver and guides who point out interesting things about the city.

Just a few steps from the cruise ship terminal and busy harbor is Gastown, one of the oldest parts of the city. It has been restored to become a lively shopping and restaurant neighborhood. This old part of town began in 1867 and was named for "Gassy Jack," a local saloon keeper who was well known as a non-stop talker. Its old streets are paved in brick and cobblestones and are crowded with sidewalk cafés. Shoppers weave among these to find stores selling uniquely Canadian crafts, antiques, and imported goods.

Costumed guides in the historic Gastown neighborhood of Vancouver

Every 15 minutes, everyone stops to watch the Steam Clock perform. This Vancouver tradition on the corner of Cambie and Water Streets is the only one of its kind in the world. The clock operates on underground steam that heats the nearby buildings. When it signals the quarter hour, its whistle is accompanied by a hissing and puffing of steam that rises from little chimneys on its iron top. A statue of Gassy Jack overlooks Maple Tree Square near Gastown's other landmark, the Europa Hotel. This unusual building is shaped like a long, narrow piece of pie to fit into its corner lot.

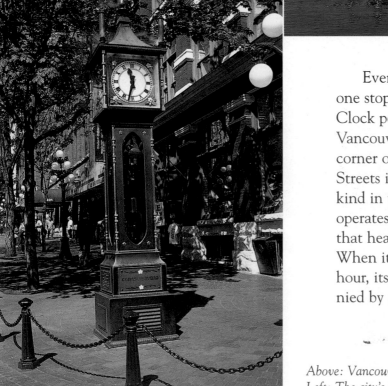

Above: Vancouver at dusk as seen from Stanley Park
Left: The city's famous Steam Clock

A PARK FOR THE PEOPLE

Stanley Park is the largest city park in North America, with 1,000 acres (405 ha) of woodland, lawns, gardens, and water. Although it adjoins the busiest part of downtown, much of its center is a wilderness of thick forests. The park was set aside in 1886, when Vancouver had only about 1,000 residents. Its founders were very forward-looking to picture the need for such a park in a town that was then surrounded by wilderness.

A paved seawall promenade surrounds the park, running along the water's edge. Throughout the park are trails, many of which were used by the Salish First Nations People who lived in several villages there. Lumberman's Arch, built to honor men in the logging trades, stands at the site of one of these Salish villages.

Today, local families and tourists alike can tour the park in horse-drawn carriages. A miniature railroad operated

Visitors enjoy touring Stanley Park in horse-drawn carriages.

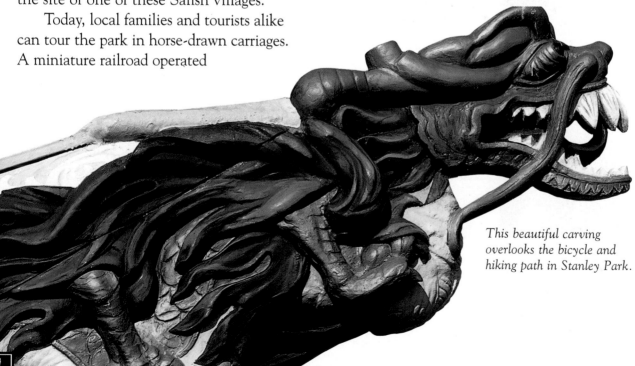

This beautiful carving overlooks the bicycle and hiking path in Stanley Park.

by a steam locomotive runs though the woods. It is one of the most popular activities in the park, running every day in the summer and on winter weekends when the weather is nice.

In the summer, Vancouver police at Kids' Traffic School teach young people about how cars and people share the streets. Children can pedal miniature cars along "streets" to learn about intersections, one-way streets, traffic lights, and how police help keep cars moving safely in Vancouver.

Two of Vancouver's favorite attractions are in Stanley Park—the Children's Zoo and the Vancouver Aquarium Marine Science Centre. Most of the zoo's animals are in a large area where children can walk right in and pet them. Dangerous animals are not kept there, of course.

The Vancouver Aquarium Marine Science Centre, which opened in

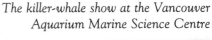

1956, was Canada's first public aquarium. It is still the largest one in Canada. Nearly 9,000 fishes, 360 amphibians, more than 50 reptiles, and about 80 birds and mammals live in and around 2.5 million gallons (9.5 million liters) of water. You might see a giant octopus, dolphins,

A jacket patch from the Vancouver Aquarium Marine Science Centre

killer whales, sea otters, sea lions, beluga whales, sharks, sloths, or giant Amazon fishes. More than just a place to see fish, the aquarium has naturalists in its galleries to help visitors understand what they see. The rehabilitation center here helps injured and abandoned sea creatures to survive.

The killer-whale show at the Vancouver Aquarium Marine Science Centre

Vancouver's Science World of British Columbia museum is inside a giant geodesic dome.

ACROSS FALSE CREEK

Little passenger ferries scuttle back and forth across False Creek, taking people between the Yaletown neighborhood and the market on Granville Island. This market is busiest on Saturdays and Sundays. That is when many people like to begin the day with breakfast in the market or at a nearby café, then browse in the shops and galleries. These are in old warehouses and industrial buildings, which have been painted bright colors and recycled into shops and eating places.

Even people who are not shopping for food like to see Granville Island Market, just for its beautiful displays of fruits, vegetables, and flowers. The farmers who sell there seem to compete with one another to see who can make the prettiest displays. They choose their most perfect fruits and vegetables and arrange them in attractive ways.

A playground called the Water Park is especially designed for summer play. It is a huge wading pool with fire hoses that children can use to spray anyone who comes within reach.

At the end of False Creek, reached by the same fleet of small ferries, is Science World of British Columbia. Its hands-on exhibits and activities include a tornado and a chance to crawl though a beaver lodge. The museum is inside a giant geodesic dome.

Left: A seafood vendor with Dungeness crabs at the Granville Market

Above: A child playing on a fire hydrant at the Granville Island Water Park

ON THE LOWER MAINLAND

The part of British Columbia where Vancouver is located is called the Lower Mainland, and it is one of Canada's most popular places to visit.

The Okanagan Valley lies along the shores of Lake Okanagan, east of Vancouver. Protected by mountains from both the northern cold and the Pacific Ocean's cool sea air, this sheltered valley is Canada's most important fruit-growing region. It is the only place in the country where apricots are grown, and it is famed for its grapes and the wines made from them. Its farms,

Skiers (below) enjoy staying in Whistler Village (above) on Whistler Mountain.

vineyards, and orchards make it a beautiful region to visit, especially in the spring when its fruit trees are in bloom.

Skiing near Vancouver is not just a sport for the middle of winter. Even on warm days in May, people ride up Whistler Mountain to ski on the glacier, then play golf or work on their tans around the swimming pool in the afternoon. The two mountains there have the highest vertical rise of any ski area in North America. The ski trails lead right into a village of shops,

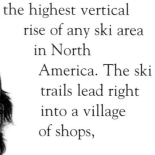

Spectacular scenery in the area of Whistler Mountain

restaurants, and hotels. It's no wonder that skiers have voted this North America's top ski destination.

The road from Vancouver to Whistler, called the Sea-to-Sky Highway, hugs the coast much of the way. The beautiful scenery along the road is a panorama of islands, water, and mountains. The small town of Britannia Beach, with only about 350 residents, once had a population of 60,000, and recalls those days with its mining museum.

VICTORIA AND VANCOUVER ISLAND

Although it is British Columtia's largest city, Vancouver is not the capital. That title goes to Victoria, a short ferry or floatplane ride south, on Vancouver Island. Don't be confused by the names: the city of Vancouver is not located on the nearby island of the same name.

Victoria is a beautiful city that reminds many visitors of England. Teatime is

Above: Victoria's Empress Hotel serves more than 1.5 million cups of afternoon tea each year.

Left: The Parliament Buildings in Victoria, the capital of British Columbia

observed each day at the grand Empress Hotel, which serves more than 1.5 million cups of afternoon tea each year. Like Vancouver, Victoria centers around its historic Inner Harbour. In fact, British Columbia's Parliament Buildings sit right next to the water.

Although it can't compare with Vancouver's in size, Victoria's Chinatown is the oldest in Canada. Victoria's streets are lined with fine old homes built in the 1800s. Several of the most historic of these have been opened as museums. The most outstanding attraction is the Royal British Columbia Museum. It brings hundreds of years of history to life with its realistic, reconstructed mining camp, fishing port, and the entire main street of a nineteenth-century town. Its First Nations gallery has beautiful totems and boxes carved and painted by the Haida.

People who live in Victoria are dedicated to their beautiful gardens, which thrive in the warm, humid climate. These gardens began with the first settlers, who were determined to carve a bit of civilization out of the wilderness they found. They planted roses, which still fill the city with fragrance and color in June. The showplace for flowers is Butchart Gardens, built to beautify an unsightly stone quarry. It is certainly successful, blooming throughout the seasons, from acres of showy daffodils in March to its late fall chrysanthemums.

More than 1.5 million people travel north of Victoria each year to see the small town of Chemainus. When this little port lost its sawmill, the main industry, people came up with a good way to bring visitors there. They invited talented artists to paint historic murals on the walls of downtown buildings. Now visitors can walk past beautiful paintings that show Chemainus since the days when First Nations Peoples fished off its shores.

An official Victoria welcomer costumed in an authentic British uniform

FAMOUS LANDMARKS

A mural at the Vancouver Maritime Museum

The Lookout! at Harbour Centre

The Grouse Mountain Skyride

Science World of British Columbia

Vancouver Aquarium Marine Science Centre
Introducing the wonders of the underwater world, the aquarium in Stanley Park has exhibits of sea life in the Pacific Northwest, Arctic Canada, the Amazon rain forests, and the Pacific tropics.

BC Place Stadium
Vancouver's professional football team, the BC Lions, plays in the 60,000-seat stadium. It is the largest air-supported, dome-covered stadium in the world. Inside is the Sports Hall of Fame, with photos, medals, and displays honoring all of British Columbia's Olympic medalist athletes since 1912.

Vancouver Museum
Inside this cone-shaped building, life-sized exhibits show the city's history. A car from the first train that brought passengers to Vancouver on the new Canadian Pacific Railway is there, and an entire trading post re-creates the city's earliest days of European settlement.

UBC Museum of Anthropology
This outstanding museum is best known for art of the Pacific Northwest's First Nations Peoples, but its varied exhibits cover far more. Its unique open-storage system means that nearly all the collections are available

for viewing. Outside are totems and two carved Haida buildings.

Lighthouse Park
Trails lead through a 187-acre (76-ha) rain forest of the Lower Mainland's largest Douglas fir trees. At the end is a working lighthouse at Point Atkinson. Bald eagles nest in the trees along the park's cliffs.

Dr. Sun Yat Sen Classical Chinese Garden
The first authentic Chinese garden constructed outside China, the Dr. Sun Yat Sen Garden in Chinatown, was built by 52 master craftsmen. In thirteen months, they completed the garden and its

buildings, using traditional methods and materials, most of which were sent from China. No nails were used in the buildings.

Vancouver Maritime Museum
The striking glass building was built around the restored ship *St. Roch*, a two-masted sailing schooner. Also in the museum are ships from other places in the world and exhibits on local seafaring.

A view of the Dr. Sun Yat Sen classical garden in Chinatown

The Vancouver Museum

Grouse Mountain Skyride
The Skyride carries passengers to the top of Grouse Mountain, where they can eat in the restaurant or just enjoy the panoramic views of the city, water, and mountains. In the winter, ski trails lead to the bottom of the mountain, which is in North Vancouver.

Steam Clock
The steam-driven clock at the corner of Cambie and Water Streets is the only one like it in the world. It marks every quarter hour with a whistle and a hissing of steam.

Canada Place
This easily recognized building with five white "sails" on top was built for Expo 86 and is now part of a waterfront complex that houses Vancouver's cruise port, a convention center, an IMAX theater, and a hotel.

Stanley Park
So close to 1,000 acres (405 ha) that most people just round it off, Stanley Park is a short walk from downtown. Almost completely surrounded by water, it has hiking and bike trails, horse-drawn carriage and train rides, a zoo and aquarium, as well as gardens and beaches.

Harbour Centre
The Lookout! at Harbour Centre resembles a flying saucer that landed on top of a skyscraper. Its round observation deck, 500 feet (152 m) above the harbor, offers views in every direction as well as displays depicting Vancouver's history.

Marine Building
When this art-deco-style building was constructed in 1930, it was the tallest building in the entire British Commonwealth of Nations. Its detailed carvings and decorations in marble, terracotta, stone, and metal represent designs of ships and boats.

Science World of British Columbia
The shining glass geodesic dome of Science World is easy to spot at the end of False Creek, near the railway station. Inside, activities invite visitors to touch and to take part as they learn about the world around them.

Capilano Suspension Bridge
This wooden planked pedestrian bridge is the oldest tourist attraction in Vancouver. It straddles the 350-foot- (107-m-) wide Capilano Canyon at a height of 230 feet (70 m). The gentle swaying of the bridge offers a thrill to visitors.

FAST FACTS

POPULATION

City: 521,000
Metropolitan area: 1,935,000

AREA

44 square miles
(113 sq km)

ALTITUDE

Sea level

LOCATION

Vancouver is at the southwest corner of the province of British Columbia, only 24 miles (39 km) north of the U.S. state of Washington. It sits on the northern shore of a delta formed by the Fraser River as it enters the Strait of Georgia, an inlet of the Pacific Ocean. Vancouver is exactly halfway between the continents of Europe and Asia.

CLIMATE

Vancouver's weather is the mildest in Canada, because the city is protected by mountains from the harsh winters of the north, and also enjoys the moderating influence of the Pacific Ocean's currents. Daytime temperatures average 70 degrees Fahrenheit (20° Celsius) in the summer and 35 degrees Fahrenheit (1.7°C) in the winter. Winter is the rainy season, with little snow in the city. Annual rainfall is 67 inches (170 cm).

ECONOMY

Vancouver has Canada's largest port, with an average of 30 ships a day entering its harbor. From May to September, more than 300 cruises call at the city, making it a major western cruise port. An international city, Vancouver welcomes more than 8 million tourists each year. Its primary industries are tourism, banking, trade, and communications.

CHRONOLOGY

1792
Captain George Vancouver charts and claims Burrard Inlet and the surrounding area for Britain.

1808
Simon Fraser follows a river now named for him and comes to the Strait of Georgia.

1827
The Hudson's Bay Company builds a fur-trading post and fort at Fort Langley.

1858
Thousands of prospectors rush to the region when gold is discovered in the sands of the Fraser River.

1858
Britain creates the Crown Colony of British Columbia, with New Westminster as its capital.

1871
British Columbia joins the Dominion of Canada.

1875
Canneries pack and process fish for shipment all over the world.

1884
The Canadian Pacific Railway decides to make the Burrard Inlet its West Coast terminus.

1886
Granville incorporates itself as the City of Vancouver.

A visitor admires one of the many totems in Stanley Park.

1888
Vancouver opens Stanley Park, its first public recreation area.

1923
British Columbia pressures the federal government to enact the Chinese Immigration Act, preventing Chinese people from entering Canada.

1949
Canadians of Chinese ancestry are granted full rights and allowed to become Canadian citizens.

1956
Canada's first public aquarium, the Vancouver Aquarium Marine Science Centre, opens.

1984
The Asia Pacific Foundation of Canada is established, with its headquarters in Vancouver.

1986
Expo 86 is held in Vancouver, bringing more than twice as many people as expected.

1995
GM Place opens, providing a home for Vancouver's hockey and basketball teams and a 22,000-seat concert hall.

VANCOUVER

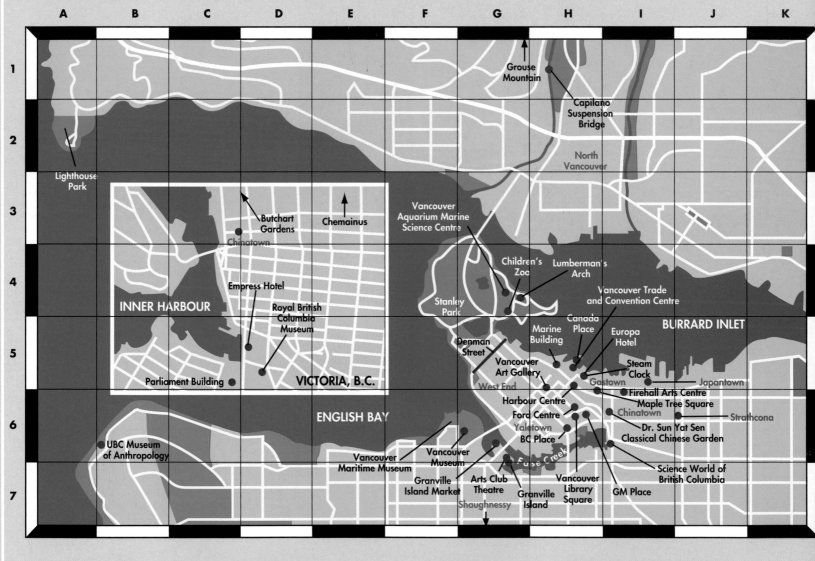

A B C D E F G H I J K

1
2
3
4
5
6
7

Grouse Mountain

Capilano Suspension Bridge

North Vancouver

Lighthouse Park

Vancouver Aquarium Marine Science Centre

Butchart Gardens

Chemainus

Chinatown

Children's Zoo

Lumberman's Arch

Vancouver Trade and Convention Centre

Empress Hotel

INNER HARBOUR

Royal British Columbia Museum

Stanley Park

Marine Building

Canada Place

Europa Hotel

BURRARD INLET

Denman Street

Steam Clock

Japantown

Vancouver Art Gallery

Gastown

Firehall Arts Centre

West End

Maple Tree Square

Parliament Building

VICTORIA, B.C.

Harbour Centre

Ford Centre

Chinatown

Strathcona

ENGLISH BAY

Yaletown

BC Place

Dr. Sun Yat Sen Classical Chinese Garden

UBC Museum of Anthropology

False Creek

Science World of British Columbia

Vancouver Maritime Museum

Vancouver Museum

Vancouver Library Square

GM Place

Granville Island Market

Arts Club Theatre

Granville Island

Shaughnessy

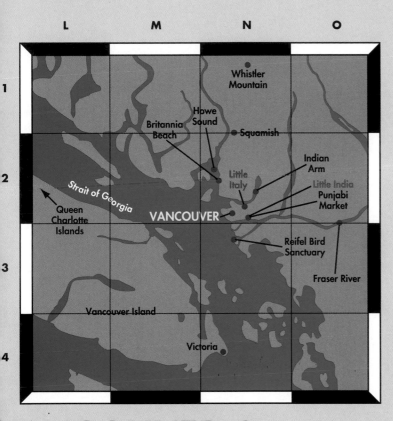

VANCOUVER & SURROUNDINGS

GLOSSARY

art deco: A style of architecture and decoration popular in the early twentieth century

British Empire: The nations and territories that once were ruled by Great Britain, including Canada, Australia, New Zealand, India, and much of Africa

delta: A triangular-shaped piece of land that builds up at a river's entrance to the sea

First Nations Peoples: Canada's Native Americans

floatplane: An airplane that lands and takes off on water

gentrifying: The process of turning a run-down older neighborhood into a fashionable place to live

Pacific Rim: The entire area around the Pacific Ocean, including Asia and western North America

schooner: A style of sailing ship, usually with two or three masts and triangular sails

transcontinental: Stretching across the continent, from the Atlantic Coast to the Pacific Coast

Picture Identifications

Cover: A view of Vancouver; a visitor approaching Vancouver by boat
Page 1: Visitors with painted faces at the Vancouver Children's Festival
Pages 4–5: Summer sunset, Coal Harbour, Vancouver
Pages 8–9: Mountains near the sea, Vancouver
Pages 18–19: An early view of Vancouver
Pages 30–31: Sunken Gardens, Butchart Gardens, Victoria
Pages 44–45: Inner Harbour, Victoria

Photo Credits ©

Al Harvey — Cover (background), 1, 12, 28 (both pictures), 32, 33 (bottom)
Travel Stock — Buddy Mays, cover (foreground), 7 (right), 10, 11 (bottom left), 37 (top), 48 (bottom), 59
KK&A, Ltd. — 3, 11 (top and bottom right), 34 (top), 36, 40 (bottom), 60, 61
Tom Stack & Associates — T. Kitchin, 4–5, 54 (bottom)
New England Stock Photo — Andre Jenny, 6 (left); John C. White, 30–31; Jean Higgins, 51 (right), 55, 56 (middle)
The Viesti Collection, Inc. — Richard Cummins, 6–7, 27, 33 (top left); Walter Bibikow, 47 (top)
Unicorn Stock Photos — Marie Mills/D. Cummings, 8–9
Wolfgang Kaehler — 13 (top), 29
Dave G. Houser — 13 (bottom), 49 (bottom); John Gottberg, 47 (bottom), 56 (left); Rankin Harvey, 53
Spectrum Stock — 54 (top); Brian Hay, 14; Bob Chambers, 17 (bottom); Tim Pelling, 33 (top right); Halby Gunby, 41 (top); Dan Fivehouse, 41 (bottom); Norman Piluke, 57 (middle)
Robert Holmes — 15 (top), 48 (top), 57 (left)
Capilano Suspension Bridge — 15 (bottom)
BC Rail — 16 (both pictures)
Corbis — 22; Michael Lewis, 17 (top); Kevin R. Morris, 21 (bottom)
Archive Photos — 18–19; Reuters/Mike Blake, 43
Corbis–Bettmann — 20
North Wind Picture Archives — 21 (top)
North Wind Pictures — 22–23, 24, 25
Tom Till Photography — 23 (right)
UPI/Corbis–Bettmann — 26 (top)
Stock Montage, Inc. — 26 (bottom)
SuperStock — George Hunter, 34 (bottom), 52 (top); Timothy Hursley, 35; D. C. Lowe, 44–45; Chigmaroff/Davison, 56 (bottom right)
Robert Fried — 37 (bottom), 51 (left), 52 (bottom)
Reuters Newmedia Inc./Corbis — 38, 42 (bottom)
Photo Edit — Richard Hutchings, 39
AP Photo — Chuck Stoody, 40 (top), 42 (top)
Visuals Unlimited — Jeff Greenberg , 46
Vancouver Aquarium Marine Science Centre — 49 (top)
Tony Stone Images, Inc. — Bob Herger, 50
Cameramann International, Ltd. — 56 (top right)

INDEX

Page numbers in boldface type indicate illustrations

TO FIND OUT MORE

BOOKS

Fodor's 2001 Vancouver and British Columbia. New York: Fodor's Travel Publications, Inc., 2001.

Goodman, Michael E. *Vancouver Grizzlies. NBA Today.* Mankato, Minn.: Creative Education, 1998.

Grabowski, John F. *Canada.* Modern Nations of the World series. San Diego: Lucent Books, 1998.

King, Jane and Andrew Hempstead. *British Columbia Handbook: Including Vancouver, Victoria, and the Canadian Rockies.* Chico, Calif.: Moon Publications, 1998.

LeVert, Suzanne and Sheppard George. *British Columbia.* Canada in the 21st Century series. New York: Chelsea House, 2000.

MacIntyre, Iain. *Vancouver Canucks.* NHL Today series. Mankato, Minn.: Creative Education, 2000.

ONLINE SITES

British Columbia – WorldWeb Travel Guide:
http://www.discoverbc.com/
A tourism and visitor guide with links to attractions and activities throughout British Columbia, including Vancouver, the Rockies, Vancouver Island, Whistler, and many other places; includes interactive maps, a photo gallery, travel and vacation information, and more.

Capilano Suspension Bridge and Park:
http://www.capbridge.com
Includes pictures and information on this amazing suspension bridge within a park that has a West Coast rain forest, colorful totem poles carved by First Nations Peoples, a story center, restaurants, and more.

Super, Natural British Columbia:
http://www.hellobc.com/index.jsp?ct=1
Features British Columbia Escapes with links to regions, cities, attractions, maps, accommodations, activities, festivals and events, travel information, and more.

Welcome to Vancouver, Canada!:
http://www.tourismvancouver.com/docs/visit/index.html
This Tourism Vancouver - Greater Vancouver Convention and Visitors Bureau site features Vancouver and its 18 surrounding municipalities. Includes information on things to do, places to stay, a calendar of events, shopping, things for children to do, entertainment, restaurants, accommodations, ways to get around, tips for traveling, boat charters, and more.

Welcome to Victoria, British Colulmbia:
http://attractionsvictoria.com/main.html
A rich site with pictures and information on a tremendouss number of Victoria attractions, including the Butchart Gardens, Craigdarroch Castle, Crystal Garden, the Empress Hotel, Fisherman's Wharf, Miniature World, galleries, museums, markets and shopping centers, parks and beaches, sports and recreation, and much more.

ABOUT THE AUTHORS
Stillman (Tim) and Barbara Rogers have written guidebooks to Canada for Thomas Cook Publishing in London and for Frommer's Guides. Most recently, they wrote the 646-page *Adventure Guide to Canada's Atlantic Provinces.* Stillman is the author of *Montreal* in the Cities of the World series and together they wrote *Toronto* in that series and *Canada* in the Enchantment of the World series, all published by Children's Press. Barbara and their daughter Lura are co-authors of *Dominican Republic* in the Enchantment of the World Series. Stillman and Barbara are the authors of books on South Africa, Zambia, and Peru for the Children of the World series.